# BEFORE THE AFTER

# BEFORE THE AFTER

Love, Loss, and Revolution in the Time of COVID

Mary Anne Anderson

First Edition

POETRY

Keyes Canyon Press
SAN MIGUEL, CALIFORNIA

## Praise for Before the After

Read this book straight through! Images in every poem build on the ones before to grow increasingly profound. Lyrical words firing wonderful images - stanza by stanza, poem by poem - dig an entrance into unexpected depth. Sometimes single words dissolved me through a floor I always saw as solid. If you want intellectual poetry, go elsewhere. For lyric poetry to enchant you - stay here - read this book! — John Calkins, author of *Dad, Demons, Dames and a Dwarf: My Trip Down Freedom Road* with Mancow Muller

Blending humor, disappointment and wisdom, Mary Anne invites us to share her travels navigating a world altered by the rise of Black Lives Matter and curtailed by COVID-19. Poetic vignettes narrate events cancelled due to the virus, an imaginative letter to humanity from a disappointed Gaia, how life during the time of coronavirus has radically changed. She explores what we have lost and how we transform and adapt — Dr. Jennifer Lagier, Author of *Camille Comes Unglued* and *Dystopia Playlist*.

Mary Anne Anderson's poems ignite an imagery of new normal forced upon us by the relentless pandemic as it permeates our lives, unmasking issues of unequal justice, police brutality and systemic racism while showing how the human spirit and social courage attempt to adapt to new normal. Her poems move around and in-between what defines us and what we do to ourselves. Her poetry is concerned with how we fail to understand one another due to bias, hate, ignorance and intolerance." — Ashok K. Bhargava, President of Writers International Network

Mary Anne Anderson takes you on an emotional journey through the COVID Virus pandemic with a poetic narrative of the artist's survival during a season of tragedy. She brilliantly threads insight and compassion and combines fierce intelligence with a bared heart in this remarkable book. — Melinda Gohn, Maui Live Poets Society, International Peace Poem Project

Published 2021

Printed in the United States of America

Before the After: Love, Loss and Revolution in the Time of COVID. -- 1st ed.

ISBN 978-0-9850074-9-2 Paperback

ISBN 978-1-7356528-0-1 eBook

Library of Congress Control Number: 2020946949

25 24 23 22 21    1 2 3 4 5

Cover design by Tony Portillo

Graphic elements from Clipartix


Keyes Canyon Press
San Miguel, CA 93451
www.keyescanyonpress.com

*Dedicated to all the essential workers (medical, postal, and delivery drivers, restaurant and grocery workers, farmers, and more) for their fortitude and loyalty; and to all those who have experienced the ravages of this terrible pandemic.*

# CONTENTS

# ACKNOWLEDGEMENTS

"Escape", "I Am Thermal King" and "The Mirror Has Two Faces" first appeared in *Treehouse Arts*: July 2020

"The Mirror Has Two Faces" and "Rewind" appeared in *Maui Muses 5*: Fall 2020

"Before the After" first appeared in *Corona Silver Linings Anthology*: December 2020

# BEFORE THE AFTER

# MARCH

# On the Cancellation of My Trip to Ireland

St. Patrick would be disappointed
having driven out all the snakes
and brought luck upon the land.

Verdant isle swarming with devil germ
now closed to all who would enter
its emerald gates,
tradition subjugated,
history be dammed.

We need each other even more now,
the blend of guitar and harp and penny whistle,
voice and harmony,
to adorn the lovely, lonely melody.

We are summoned to respond,
obliged to laugh,
to cry,
to sing.

# Storm Warning

The wind chimes in my garden issue a storm warning.
I run beneath a jasmine-covered trellis.
At first, benevolent raindrops descend
like salt from a shaker.
The sweet night bloomer swells, overtakes me,
its silent sleep interrupted.

The chimes rattle, louder this time.
Hollow rods of steel dangle from the tree limb,
bleat like unhappy beasts.

A gust of wind stings my face.
The trellis rattles.
Innocent jasmine flowers scatter like snowflakes
sacrificed to the tempest.

# ABC's of a Brave New World

A
acute respiratory distress syndrome
anti-viral medication
apex

B
bleach
blood tests
breathing difficulty

C
cancellations
community transmission
COVID-19

D
deaths
disinfectant
distance

E
existential threat
exponential
exposure

F
face masks
Fauci
fever

Twenty more letters and counting. . .

# Requiem

I loved you beyond reason,
beyond time,
beyond what rational thinking would allow.

I loved the Chopin in you,
your heavy eyelids,
your golden
Gershwin smile,

the way your shoulders rounded as you
leaned into the piano,
breathless,
waiting for your heart to
open,

the way your fingers glided
up and down my arm
when we slept,
as if I were your keyboard,
the way dreams rested on your lips,
mute and open.

I loved the song in you I could not hear,
the heart you could not give me,
the life you would not share.

I loved you beyond hope,
beyond goodbye.

# Third World War

Enemy unseen,
the culprit
a harsh beauty
crowned with floral clusters
clinging to a poisonous orb,
half-decorated
Styrofoam Christmas ornament
wiggling its way into our lungs.

Unmerciful slayer
with its fitful might
whose furious reproduction
eclipses missing masks and gloves.

Pity those panic-stricken
who hoard toilet paper,
fear civilization's demise,
the existential threat.

How many times must we wash our hands,
observe social distance?
We cannot wish away the strain.

Take shelter all who are
compromised.
Quarantine.
This is not a drill.

## The New Normal

Peace signs:
Remember when we were hippies and chanted,
"All you need is Love"?
We gave peace a chance, but look where are now.
A new war sprouted up and we can't even see the enemy.

Touch:
Hey I'd love to kiss both your cheeks like the French do,
but. . .
What to do when your child gets a boo-boo?
Not tonight honey, I have a headache.

Vulcan greeting:
Spock was right all along.
No tears.
Ignore that deep dark place we're in and soldier on.

Namaste greeting:
The divine in me recognizes and bows
to the divine in you.
Ommmmmmm.
Breathe in, breathe out, like the ventilator.

Body Language:
Stand six feet away.
Smiles don't cost extra.
Just keep waving.

But we can still:
Talk louder.
Cry openly.
Blow kisses.

# APRIL

# Dear Human Race

Mother Earth here.
I've been trying to reach you
for the longest time.
You do realize that I birthed you
and care for you.

Why can't you behave like good children?
Do I have to remind you again and again
to wash off that soot?

And please stop bickering over
who gets the most goodies.
The trees, the oils and minerals
the food supplies
are for all of you to share.
Please kids,
pick up your litter.
And clean up your rooms for heaven's sake.

You act as if you don't care.
Really?
This time you'll be sorry.
You'll regret soiling me so badly
I can never get rid of the stains.
And the way you've cut off my air supply,
shame on you!
You kids deserve a spanking
Maybe I should flood you with my tears again.
Or give you a good shake.

Goodness knows I've tried to warn you.

Go ahead,
keep pummeling me with your drills,
burden me with too much weight,
burn away the hair on my skin.
You can't run and you can't hide.
You'll pay for this,
my undeserving progeny.

I can wipe you out with a single sneeze.
Better yet,
let a rogue germ do it for me.
I'll just sit back and watch you perish.
I can always make other children,
ones more deserving of my bounty.

Unless. . . unless. . .
hmmm. . .
let me think.

Okay,
go to your rooms,
cover your faces in shame.
Isolation.
That ought to do it for now.
This is your last time out.

Sincerely,
Gaia

# Lament for Our Mother Earth

We have consumed
beyond our needs,
taken more than Gaia could give us.

We have ravaged her,
stripped her of her skin,
punched and prodded,
overburdened,
undernourished.

No wonder
she's trying to shake herself free
from our hold,
our greedy hands,
our dirty feet.

Tread softly
lest we all sink into
the dark eternal abyss,
the twilight's last gleaming.

# A Walk in Good Company (to John Prine)

My old dog knows the way
up and down the path
nestled in the grove of trees.

I mute the outside world,
headphones turned up
to stave off my hunger for a gentle touch
from anyone but the ghosts.

I sing along with John Prine,
his voice a mighty sound burst,
gruff yet tender.
He tells of Sam Stone,
of lovers and cheaters,
an angel from Montgomery.

We pass a mound of stones,
slabs of granite where hobos once camped,
the plaque on a wooden bench
a simple reminder of a bygone railroad depot
now a cluster of weeds and dirt.

I am in good company.
Godiva
- the chocolate-drop pup with golden eyes
I brought home from the shelter -
sniffs and trots and stops to sniff some more,
leash dragging behind her.

More song-stories echo
through the tunnel of trees.

Harmonies mingle in the wings
waiting for the chorus like holy communion.

I say, "Hello in there,"
to the old oaks, the phantom hobos
the ancestral stones, my faithful dog.

# Good Friday/Bad Friday

Absent angels,
prayers unanswered,
the splintery wooden cross
a holy remnant to remind us
of His suffering.
        Good Friday, you say?

Penitents plead for mercy
and for water
to extinguish their perpetual thirst,
cleanse the soul.
        Life everlasting, you say?

This Easter we sequester,
cannot receive the host,
drink the wine,
taste the blood
of the God-Man who promised
redemption, resurrection.
        The Rapture, you say?

Deliver us from this
madness-inducing panic.
Distract us from ourselves again,
our purpose,
with food and wine and chocolate,
so that we may forget that on this day,
the meek will not inherit the earth,

the weak will perish.
     Blessed are the merciful, you say?

Blessed are the brave,
the unyielding,
the Angel replacements
who choose duty over self,
the ones who wear masks
as their crosses.

# Watermelon Jubilee

Queen of summer,
we celebrate your power
to sate,
our tongues ready for the quenching.

Your tender belly
melts like a snow cone
as we siphon your elixir,
your sweet pink juice trickling down
our sun-dried cheeks.

I can hardly wait for summer's heat
to ripen you,
plump and replete
with liquid joy
when we can all come out again
to play.

# The Mirror Has Two Faces

The Way I Feel It:

It's hard to sleep.
Dark dreams with their
continual loop
would baffle even the absurdist.

Dreams beyond imagining
that cast me down the rabbit hole,
repeat,
then repeat backwards.

Here they come again
in my waking hours
like gargoyles licking their lips
hungry for the taste of
blood and fear.

The Way You Cope:

You sink into dreamless sleep,
no motion,
only quiet breaths
soft like the blush of sunrise.

The moon hides behind
the dawn,
no comfort required.
A bright new day awaits
with blurred periphery.

Breakfast as usual.
Sameness sedates you,
routine your escape hatch.
You write down "strawberries"
on the yellow note pad

# April Again Already

Repeat after me:
        Monday
        Tuesday
        April
        April
        April.

It's the little things:
        footsteps on the sidewalk
        church choirs
        full calendars
        children in the park
        handshakes.

Missing:
        birthday parties
        proms
        funerals
        baseball
        N-95s.

The Count:
        unemployment rates
        closed businesses
        crowded beaches
        souls lost
        tears shed.

# MAY

## Haiku

One tomato left.
Save it for a rainy day.
Did you feel those drops?

# I Am Thermo King

Top of the line
in refrigerated trucks,
reinforcement
for the overflow
in the dark quiet
behind the hospital.

My load is heavy,
my drivers tired,
heads bowed,
fingers locked in almost-prayer
as the attendants roll
gurney after gurney
into the loading zone.

The air is thick with silence,
my ice-coldness a blessing
as the stony remains
spend the in-between time
in frozen peace
while their souls depart.

# Escape

Give me a comedy,
give me sex,
give me anything to get me out
of this rut.

Pills,
thrills,
calla lilies,
sloppy kisses.

Give me good hair,
fresh pajamas,
sunshine,
red wine,
music to tap my feet to,
songs of joy,
songs of prayer.
This mama's 'bout ready to explode
with a hippity-hop,
bop-shoo-bop.

Can't try on shoes,
can't stop in for tea,
no one to sit with,
nothing fits.
Come blow me a kiss.
I won't tell if you won't.
Let's have some virtueless fun.
I'll undress if you will.
You go first.

# Take Two

All you had to say was,
"I'm sorry,"
before the flood of complaints
oozed out of my pores.

All you had to do was
come close,
apologize,
tell me you'll do better next time.

But no,
when your defense shields flashed
and you postured for a fight,
I fought back,
a trail of grievances following
in ghostly procession.

So where are we now?
I sulk in my corner,
you in yours,
until one of us sighs,
then yells,
"Ollie Ollie In Come free!"

# New World Order

Mommy, what's this?

*It's called Lipstick.*

What's lipstick?

*That's something women once used to paint their lips, to look pretty.*

But you can't see lips through the masks.

*That's right, dear. Not any more.*

So how do they look pretty now? I mean, without lipstick.

*It's in the eyes. The way you look at someone, the way you smile.*

But I thought you could only smile with your mouth.

*Oh, no. There's much more to a smile than that.*

Mommy, what's a classroom?

*A room where children learned together.*

Like we learn on our tablets?

*Yes, but children were all in the same room.*

Close to each other?

*Yes, and they played sports at recess.*

What's recess?

*The time when children went outdoors to play.*

All together?

*Yes, together.*

Mommy, what's a handshake?

*That's something people used to do to say hello.*

How?

*They grasped their hands together and moved them up and down.*

But that's dangerous, isn't it?

*Now it is, yes. But in the olden days, people were much closer physically.*

Why?

*Because humans need physical touch and contact.*

# JUNE

# Sports Deprived

We sit in front of the TV screen
late night channel surfing,
eyes glossy,
half a beer resting on the coffee table,
our fingers entwined like knotted oak limbs.

The boys of summer are stranded this year.
Weeds sprout around the bases.
Withdrawal has him in its clutch:
no whoosh of fastballs,
grace of sliders,
din of crowds to lull him to sleep.
He needs his lullaby.

Fatigue hovers like a dark cloud
that won't burst.
Another classic replay over.
The home team won.
He's as happy as he was
back in ninety-two.

Midnight has swallowed us whole.
He changes channels,
mutes the TV,
yawns into the heavy silence.
On the screen
two men stand side by side
and toss something
into a slanted board.

What are we watching now?
Cornhole.
What's that?
They throw a sack of corn into a hole.

I shake my head.

# They Were Just Following Orders

When Caesar commanded his soldiers
across the shallow waters of the Rubicon
and the die was cast;

When Crusaders took up the holy cross,
their pilgrimage a promise of redemption
as they ravaged Jerusalem;

When Custer and his men,
determined to preserve their race,
rode head first into the slaughter;

When Nazis stuffed Jews into cattle cars
and delivered them to their final destination
where they turned on the gas spigots;

When state troopers unleashed attack dogs in Selma,
National Guardsmen shot students at Kent State,
and federal authorities teargassed protesters
in Washington D.C.
to clear the way for a photo op.

# G-E-O-R-G-E  F-L-O-Y-D Syndrome

Going somewhere, boy?

> *Every day the same question.*

> *On whose authority do you ask?*

Righteousness be damned, nigger. What's your name?

> *Get offa' my case, man. I ain't botherin' nobody.*

> *Even if I told you, would it matter?*


For Christ sake boy, you looking for a fight?

> *Listen Mister Police man. I'm no saint, but I got rights.*

Oh, you got that wrong. Hands up! You're under arrest.

> *You kidding me?*
Dead serious.

# Five Black Cherries

Back in the day,
mother never asked me
what color he was,
where his parents came from,
or what he planned to do
with his young and fruitful life.

No.
She simply asked,
"Does he care for you?"

I can still hear her question today.
"Oh yes," I reply.
"He brings me tea
and five black cherries
every night after dinner."

# Blacklash

I felt the belt but not the whip.
After weeks, welts left no marks,
but the memory planted itself into my soul
like a weed that all the therapy in the world
could not eradicate.

The lashes they gave your forebears sank deeper,
scars like tattoos, reminders of your subjugation,
generations of memories etched into you like
uninvited DNA.

I do not fear suppression.
I walk the street protected by my
armor of whiteness
while you, my sister, always on the lookout,
avoid recognition when sirens blare,
your streets peppered with shell casings.

Head down, quick-footed,
your safety net torn to shreds,
you give your son "the talk,"
braid your daughter's hair,
warn them of the dangers of wearing
the dark skin they cannot shed.

And when you rise up,
take the whip into your hands and swing
so that I may feel the lash of your blackness.

# Before the After

Before awareness, the waters knew,
their tides swelled a slow-stirring
undertow, underfoot,
while we frolicked and splashed
floating weightless on the shores of oblivion.

Before awakeness, the wind retreated,
held its breath,
gasped,
then let out a single, sorry sigh,
spewing dust and time-drenched molecules
— the perfect storm.

Before aliveness, the soul journeyed
the earth and beyond,
knew its purpose:
to survive, to thrive, to do no harm
then to become immortal.

Before sickness, germs gathered,
united soldiers of revenge,
as if to say,
    *You fools, you silly selfish lot,*
but we carried on,
met face to face
while they sprinkled their poison like fairy dust.

Before darkness spread its velvet blanket
over us like a shroud,
peeled off the color from our faces,
white blindness struck like a lightning bolt,
thrust us toward the burning sun.

# Missing

There's something about the sound
that's missing,
hearing the voice,
the spoken heart,
feeling the poem's pulse,
the written word begging
to find a home on the page,
resurrect on some poet's lips,
but for the mask.

# JULY

# Unholy Mount

The crackle and pomp of independence,
boisterous cheers unmuted by masks,
the feckless crowd applauds
four faces carved in stone,
one on the ground spewing vitriol,
heedless of the hazardous embers
that threaten the Ponderosa pines.

Sacred ground to the Lakota Sioux,
hills black and scarred with shame.
Dynamite and drills
shattered rocks of ages ago,
now a tribute to the abusers,
truth and comfort blown away
like sand in a desert.

We, who declared ourselves free from tyranny,
from subjugation,
we who enslaved, who removed the indigenous
peoples from their lands,
we, still shackled by possession and greed,
soiled with the stains of slavery,
we the people
celebrate what?

Freedom?

# Rewind

Out from the valley of yesterday
we trudge,
one foot outstretched,
the other stuck in place.

The road ahead twists and teases,
then yanks us backwards
like a taut rubber band.

Weariness weighs heavy
in the absence of time.
Dry bones creak and complain,
the promise of tomorrow thwarted,
hours and days reduced to seconds
on a clock that will not tick.

# We'll Always Have Maui

In February we began to count.
Winter took its last bite of sun from the cold
grey plate of clouds,
suitcase of memories still unpacked.

Awake in palm tree dreams
the crunch of wet sand
still ringing in our ears,
white powder beach clinging to our toes,
March yawned, took its time
then disappeared without a trace of regret.

Six weeks, five, thirty days 'til our homecoming.
Captives of anticipation,
we welcomed April like a newborn.
Nineteen days away, eighteen. . .

Delay,
more delay,
unanswerable questions,
slow motion nothingness.

Our Valley Isle's fire flickers in the dim light,
ghost of might-have-beens.
She waits for us on the other side of tomorrow,
locked in the prison of time.

The sweet scent of her plumeria
has not drifted into the forgotten past,
nor have the memories faded,
the memories we lean on
when the fog sets in,
memories resting in the azure sky,
the bamboo forests,
*honu** lounging on the shoreline.

Maui waits for us
like a woman waits for her beloved,
eyes aglow with verdant light,
waits, as always,
for the curse to lift,
the tide to change.

And with a loving sigh
she smiles,
strums a soft *mele**,
holds us in her sway.

* *honu* - turtles
* *mele* - song

# Mask Media

We have masks.
Free shipping.
Buy two and save.

We have tie-dye,
watermelon,
smiles and smirks,
flag masks,
zebra masks
magenta,
lime green,
celestial skies,
polka dots,
whatever suits your mood.

Express yourself.
What does the mask say about you?
You're fierce, friendly,
a Leo, a Pisces,
a Dodgers fan.

A smile, a frown,
a flower, a clown.
Who says you can't be all of these?

Order now!

# Un-Presidented Times

Rudderless ship of state,
filled with fools who know not
the navigation of the stars,
celestial bodies that point toward safe harbors.

They ride the oceans' swells and dips,
the storm thirsty for their souls,
its eye upon them, on their heels,
rending them apart with its
turbulence, eager to
crush their bones.

Ahoy!
Assemble!
Thrust your oars forward
into the eye of Cyclops,
into the belly of the whale.

Trust no one, ask and answer
your own questions
while on the deck, no captain lies
fallen cold and dead.

Instead, he cowers on the shore,
behind the mask a puckered face,
a crooked smile,
the amphibian who cannot swim,
claws clinging to the sand.

# One Hundred Days

April 17th, one hundred days ago: belated April Fools!
Thirty thousand, two hundred ninety-six American souls
already snatched away by the virus. "We have passed the
peak in new cases," *he* said, while New York's victims
amounted to over twelve thousand.

> counting the numbers
> not the beings
> statistics cannot calm the weary

Governors had to fend for themselves. Nurses fell sick.
One insurance group's profits grew by over a hundred
and fifty million dollars. I was spitting out poems like sun-
flower seeds at a baseball game, only there was no
baseball. I sheltered in place, then walked alone along the
bluffs, on country roads, five, six miles a day, storybooks
in my ears.

> one hundred days ago
> the vague haze of uncertainty
> a certainty

July 26th, one hundred days to go: The "little flu" has
plucked one hundred fifty thousand, two hundred eighty-
three souls from our disunited states. Finally, *he* dons a
mask. Refrigerated trucks are full to capacity, ICU's

crowded with party-goers who dared to dance too close, now silenced by ventilators.

> drone of life support
> pumping of oxygen
> into disobedient lungs

George Floyd is dead. Roger Stone and Michael Cohen are free. The secret police are clamping down on Portland, gas masked, unidentified. Cities ablaze, citizens rage. Businesses are closed again, many for good. We wait for guidance, wait for a cure, wait for someone, anyone, to take the helm, one hundred days from now.

> John Lewis's final crossing
> the clop of horses' hooves a rally cry
> to make good trouble

# Isolation

The solitary spider waits inside
its elegant threads,
blood-thirsty and patient.

Zygiella Orb web dangles,
bounces from the tips of pointy leaves
and with each wind breath
invites my fingers
or another creature
to touch its gauzy silk,
taste the spider's sting,
unable to retreat.

My garden fence wraps itself around me.
The flora, an orb within an orb,
the phantom shield a spectrum of greens
dancing about like a school girl with new shoes.

Unlike the spider, I welcome human touch,
but for the danger in it.
Isolation is my safety net.
No silky threads. Instead,
bolts of heavy branches
bedecked in green density
keep me at a safe distance.

# AUGUST

# Lightning Bugs

Grandmother Peg poked little holes on the lids
of five glass jars,
one for each of us.
My sister and the cousins and I
counted the minutes 'til darkness set in
and we could go on the hunt.

One by one, tiny twinkling lights
teased us all around the back yard,
past the swings, the badminton net,
the soft dewy grass of a Delaware August
between our toes.

We chased, squealed, jumped
and shouted each time somebody caught one,
the lightning bugs bottled up inside the jars,
sparkles of light flickering on and off
in our little world.

After the count, whoever captured the most
got the first ice cream cone.
I always came in last.

Later, just before bed,
I tiptoed outside to set mine free.

# The Plea

Allow me my hour of release.
I'm checking out for now.
The time has come for me to be accountable
to no one but myself,
corpus liberum *.

The muse has poured her silver elixir
into the top of my head,
its lid open to receive the holy wafer of inspiration.
My arms undulate to the music I alone can hear
as if under water, under the influence of freedom.

I dance and swing, fling my limbs about,
not a beat out of rhythm,
nothing out of place.
Euterpe has her way with me,
settles in like an ancient fairy whose wings
have not forgotten their weightlessness
as she flits about and traverses
the land of my imagination.

Allow me this respite
in the in-between,
where pain and poetry diverge
and poetry wheels me home.

*corpus liberum – body-free

# Just Like Hotel California

Hey kid, wanna party?
Take the first left at the top of the hill.
Parking $10.
Leave the keys.

The rest of the gang's hanging by the pool.
Hot chicks and cool dudes lift their glasses,
bump and grind in the water,
music blaring, decibels be dammed.
Are you having fun yet?

It's all hoax, you know,
just old folks dying.
Their number's up soon anyway.
More room on the planet.

There's a girl in the jacuzzi with a nice tan
and a rose tattoo on her shoulder
who's trying too hard
not to make eye contact,
but you know she's looking.

Kegs of beer and shots of tequila,
nachos galore and coke in the corner,
people move in closer, huddle in the pool
to rinse off the sweet summer sweat.
All the pretty boys hover under poolside umbrellas,
six pack abs and speedos on display.
You've still got your eyes on the bronze beauty.

This party's in full swing.
You could stay here forever,
and that's exactly what you'll do.
You see, we've got your keys,
and the exit is boarded up.

# Naked Ladies

They cluster by the roadside,
lean into the fog-cloaked
afternoon of no shadows,
greet me as I amble,
safely in my solitude,
lungs eager to inhale the same freedom.

The ladies tilt in close company
like ballerinas *en pointe.*
Slender stems compete for height.
Nothing can mute the wind song
as they stretch skyward.

Their watercolor blush,
silent pleas unheard,
unmasked blossoms a sacrificial offering
to a truant god,
beheaded with each snip of the shears.

## Joselyn Center Closed

. . . until further notice, the crooked sign in the window
stirs up regret
for the unattended classes, clubs dismissed as
not my kind of thing,
every stranger's face forgotten.

The empty building swathed in solitude,
phantom footsteps echo through the halls,
wait in limbo to reunite with voices,
dancers, writers, mahjong mavens.

Town hub darkened, heartbeat flatlined,
where do we go now
to laugh, to cry, to compete,
to feel complete?

# Twisted Redux

My analyst called me to say she was closing up shop.
The way she described it, she said it was best to drop
us all.
She couldn't cope with all this mess,
the Covid outbreak has caused too much distress
and she said it was best
before she ended up depressed
herself, oh no, oh no.

My herbalist told me that I should take lavender baths.
It would be so soothing
but all I could do was laugh
it off.
What did he know, how could he help
when all the astounding reviews found on Yelp
were just written by friends.
Was he a phony in the end?
Oh, yes, I guess, I guess.

They say all the children have to go back to school
but I just cannot agree.
You see this distance learning thing
is better than nothing.
They don't understand that genius kids
learn better on Zoom
where they don't have to share the room.

Well I heard that the CDC is going to pot.
That's what you get when there's no help from the top.
And poor Doctor Fauci, he was muffled and strained,
and all the time he warned us
how to deal with this plainly.
Do you think he was wrong then?
He may have telling the truth but who believed him?

They all laughed at dear Doctor Birx
and all of the neck scarves that embellished her shirts.
But why should I believe her and the dumb idiotic logic
That the POTUS tried to sell us.
Oh please give me a break.
So that's when I decided just to shelter in place.
It really is the only way
to clean up this mess, I guess.

The scientists tell me to cover my face when I sneeze.
The virus is fatal, but teenagers do as they please
and still
the party's on and the bars are filled.
There's music galore and the vodka is chilled.
Oh please give me another break.
This is such a big mistake.
Oh yes, oh dear, oh yes

My analyst told me that all of my problems are moot.
The whole world is crazy and that if I need to toot
again, just leave a message loud and clear
and try to dispel all this panic and fear
with a shot of vermouth.

And what she told me was the truth.

But you know two shots are better than one!

*"Twisted" original song lyrics by Annie Ross, recorded by Lambert, Hendrix and Ross, and made popular by Joni Mitchell.

# 'Til the Well Runs Dry

*"You don't miss your water 'til your well runs dry." William Bell*

The well, where Jesus met the woman
who tried to lie about her five husbands,
the scent of more than one man
still reeking from her,
hair the color of the raven,
eyes blackened with kohl.

The well, the one source
where women whispered secrets
shared their dreams,
drowned the unspoken.

The well, the heart center,
whose bounty went un-noticed
until it was too late.

The well, the source extinguished,
bitter aftertaste of neglect,
now an arid echo chamber,
rubble of war,
waterless hole in an empty village.

# The Reluctant Patriot

In 1971, I left my country. A senseless war had so many young souls. My generation tried to change the world by example, with love, with music. Our protests fell on deaf ears. And when my cousin Jerry was killed, I was gone for good. I wasn't alone.

> kindred spirits
> searching for answers
> when there were none

I wandered with minstrels, draft dodgers, and free spirits who crowded the Paris streets. These were my people: expats, living on bread and cheese, apples and wine. Citizens of the world, we called ourselves, beholden to no government, without a country to call home. I ran away because I could, just like the other kids, privileged, unencumbered.

> maple leaf on my backpack
> I passed for Canadian
> to hide my identity

Fifty years later, and I still don't feel American. I tried to make my country livable, free from economic suppression, from the curse of racism, ignorance, and hate. I voted for the first time in decades. Obama was the phoenix whose wings were clipped by my fellow Americans. And now we're drowning in the swamp.

> Searching for a new covenant
> so that when I make the pledge
> I mean it.

# This is Not the End

A sacred flaw has bestowed upon us
unexpected unity.
I never knew my neighbor
until he bled at my doorstep,
unmasked and alone.
Blessings come in thorny packages
but who would open them willingly?

The "if only" factor irrelevant,
the why and wherefore
washed away with our tears
leaving us to ponder the difference
between light and darkness
when we are lost in obscurity.

This is not the end.
The life cycle continues
with or without us,
ignores our pleas for mercy
and a few more years
on this uneven playing field.

And still we gather
together or distanced
on our soul-fed journey,
lift up our voices and sing,
raise our arms in prayer,
asking that the one-way winged return
we all must make
will bring us peace.

## Many Thanks To:

Ames Anderson, my ever-patient husband, whose love fills my heart with song; my fellow Cambria Writers Workshop members, who guided me through this maze of emotions with their support and helpful critique; Laura Bayless, my go-to poetry goddess; my Fellini sisters Evelyn Kahan and Barbara Barnes, who always took my late night phone calls; Susie Hansen, my best girlfriend in the whole wide world; the wild and wacky Maui Live Poets, especially Melinda Gohn and Wide Garcia; and my friends and family, who love the poet in me even if they're not crazy about poetry.

# ABOUT THE AUTHOR

Mary Anne Anderson's poem, "Ocean Walk" won first prize at the Marina, California Arts Festival, and in 2014 she received a Distinguished Poet Award from the Writers International Network in Vancouver, B.C. She belongs to the Cambria Writers Workshop and is also a member of Maui Live Poets Society. Mary Anne hosts Poetry/Spoken Word readings in her home town of Cambria, CA and divides her time between there and Maui.

A critically acclaimed singer and performer, she says of poetry: "It's where my soul sings to me." Her works appear in: VIVACE, Equitude, Plentitude of Poets, Solo Novo, Homestead Review, Drabble, First Literary Review, Treehouse Arts, Front Porch Magazine, and Maui Muses 5.

Follow Mary Anne on Facebook @
https://www.facebook.com/mary.a.anderson.543

CPSIA information can be obtained
at www.ICGtesting.com
Printed in the USA
LVHW010030150121
676462LV00006B/902

9 780985 007492